CELTIC PRAYERS AND REFLECTIONS

To my husband Ken
who shares our Pilgrimage to Celtic Holy Places

Celtic Prayers and Reflections

by
Jenny Child
with a Foreword by
David Adam

the columba press

First published in 2008 by
the columba press
55A Spruce Avenue, Stillorgan Industrial Park,
Blackrock, Co Dublin

Designed by Bill Bolger
Origination by The Columba Press
Printed in Ireland by ColourBooks Ltd, Dublin

ISBN 978 1 85607 592 3

Contents

Foreword *by David Adam*   7

Introduction   9

Part One: Our Daily Pilgrimage

Morning Prayers   10

Prayers during the Day   12

Night Prayers   16

Occasional Prayers   20

Special Intentions:

  For Patience   26

  For God's Assurance   27

  For Protection   30

  When Depressed   34

  For Inner Peace   36

  For Forgiveness   40

  For Creativity / Openness to God   43

  In Sorrow   49

  For Perseverance   52

  In Praise   56

  In Thanksgiving   59

  For God's Guidance   60

  Caring for Others   64

  For the Church   67

  For World Peace   68

Part Two

Eucharist   70

Part Three

Creation   72

Inspired by Lindisfarne   84

Part Four: Prayers through the Year

Advent	86
Christmas	89
New Year	97
Lent	98
Easter	102
Pentecost	104
All Saints	106
Blessings	109

Foreword
by David Adam

Here are prayers from the heart and the hearth. In the great tradition of Celtic prayers these are very much prayers and reflections from the ordinary daily round and from the home. There are uplifting moments and anxious moments, there are inspirational times and times of sorrow and repentance. Some prayers read like hymns, and could easily be sung, others search the heights and depths of our faith. In all we are allowed to share in the daily experiences that lead Jenny to be aware of her God.

Though I could and would be happy to use many of these prayers within a service, they are essentially prayers to be used in our own personal devotions. They are prayers to inspire us to use our own words and to bring our hopes and our fears openly before our God. Jenny's prayers are to encourage us to be at home with God and to rejoice that God is at home with us.

I commend these prayers to you as a sincere attempt to express that God is with us and in him we live and move and have our being.

Introduction

How often in our busy 21st century lifestyle do we feel we want to be somewhere 'far from the madding crowd'? Each one of us needs a place to which we can retreat to recharge our spiritual batteries, where we can stop and listen and spend time with the One who knows us best – God our Creator.

We may have a quiet refuge in our minds or somewhere real which we can visit. My special place is the Holy Island of Lindisfarne – a tidal island in Northumbria in north-east England.

It is here that both Aidan and Cuthbert, two of the early Celtic saints, lived their lives in service to God and their fellow beings. Here the seals still sing near St Cuthbert's Island and many species of birds find a safe haven.

It is my hope that you too will find your special place where you can be alone with God and experience the beauty of his Creation.

Jenny Child

Morning Prayers

A New Day
As I wake from sleep, rouse me,
   As I wash, cleanse me,
As I dress, gird me with your power,
   As I eat, energise me,
As I journey, protect me,
   As I relax, calm me,
As I sleep, surround me.

Morning Mist
As the morning mist shrouds the river
and is then lifted by the gentle rays of the rising sun,
so may our clouded spirits be raised
by the warmth of your love.

This Day and Every Day
I arise today
in your strength to uplift me,
in your power to direct me,
in your love to enfold me,
in your wisdom to guide me,
in your way to lead me
this day and every day.

A New Day
King of brightness,
you turn darkness into light
and open the shutters on a new day.
You refresh our bodies with sleep
and waken us to face
the challenges of a new dawn.
Help us to live this day to your glory.

Prayers during the Day

A Retreat

Lord, I want to be an island
  cut off by the tide,
or a castle with a moat
  and drawbridge lifted high.

Lord, I want to shut myself away
  from the stress of daily life,
and spend some time in pastures green,
  far from the toil and strife.

But, you call me to be open
  to all this day's demands
and leave whate'er the future holds
  entirely in your hands.

Enfolding Love

God the Father,
  enfold us with your love;
God the Son,
  surround us with your presence;
God the Spirit,
  revitalise us with your power.
Surround, enfold, revitalise us
  each day, each night.

Through the Day

As the sun scatters the mist
at the dawning of a new day,
So you calm our fears and anxieties
if we trust you.
You give us strength and courage
to live our daily lives
knowing you are with us
and we do not walk alone.
As the midday sun warms us,
we feel your protecting arms around us
and sense your loving presence.
As the sun sinks in a kaleidoscope of colour
you give us hope and renewal.

From Day to Day

From the dawning of the day through the morning,
guide us,
from the noontide to the setting of the sun,
lead us,
from the evening till we sleep,
keep us,
through the night till daybreak,
protect us,
and all for your love's sake.

Lord of the Day

Lord of the sunrise,
    we give thanks for the birth of each child,
    for the freshly opening rose,
    for all newborn animals.

Lord of the morning,
    we give thanks for energy and enthusiasm,
    for the challenges of a new day,
    for your Resurrection power.

Lord of the noonday,
    we give thanks for the ability to work,
    for all we can achieve,
    for unrealised potential.

Lord of the sunset,
    we give thanks for those who have died
    in the faith of Christ,
    for all who have inspired us, for our loved ones.

Lord of the night,
    we give thanks for rest and refreshment,
    for all your love and care,
    for the promise of a new day.

Comings and Goings

In our coming and going,
    guide us,
in our living and our being,
    protect us,
in our seeing and our hearing,
    enrich us,
in our thinking and our speaking,
    inspire us,
in our arriving and our departing,
    preserve us.

Be With Us

Be with us, Lord,
in our working and our resting,
in our laughing and our crying,
in our eating and our fasting,
in our travelling and our staying.
Abide with us, each day, each night.

Christ above me

Christ above me,
    Christ before me,
Christ behind me,
    Christ around me,
this day, this night,
    each day, each night.

Night Prayers

From Darkness to Light
From the darkness of night,
you wake us,
from the mire of sin,
you save us,
into your image,
you make us.

Night Prayer
I will lay down and rest
in your safety,
your angels surrounding me,
your love enfolding me,
your Spirit guarding me,
this night and every night.

Guard and Protect Us
Lighten our darkness this night, O God
and protect us with your presence;
guard us with your holy angels
and keep us from all that is evil.

God of Light
God of light,
you illuminate the night
with the radiance
of your presence.
Be with those who suffer pain
in the silent hours of darkness.
Comfort the dying and those
who watch with them.
Stay the hands of those
who are bent on evil deeds.
Give refreshing rest to those
who toss and turn in sleeplessness,
and give peace to your world.

Stay with Us
Stay with us, Lord, for the night falls
and we need your presence to gladden our hearts.
May we know you in your word
and in the breaking of bread and
the sharing of wine,
as did your Emmaus-bound disciples.
Help us to lie down in peace and sleep,
secure in your care.

Circle Me
Circle me this night
with your protection, O God.
May Christ the Saviour
surround me with his presence.
May the Holy Spirit
guard me while I sleep.
And may your holy angels
keep watch over me.

Into Your Hands
Into your hands, I commit myself this night.
May the hours of darkness hold no harm for me.
Keep me as the apple of your eye
and cover me with your protecting wings.

For Slumber
Lord,
you bring down the curtain of night on a weary world.
Help us to commit our unfinished tasks into your hands
and lay our burdens at your feet.
Grant us refreshing sleep
that we may rise in the power of Christ,
to greet another day.

The Chalice of Grief

Draw near to those, O Man of Sorrows,
who drink from the chalice of grief this night.
You who knelt in agonised prayer
in the garden of Gethsemane,
know the pain of human loss
and the anguish of sorrow.

Occasional Prayers

From Beginning to End
From the rising of the sun to its setting,
   you guide us,
from our birth to our death,
   you lead us,
in our grief and in our sorrow,
   you comfort us,
in our joy and celebration,
   you uplift us,
from the beginning of our lives to their ending,
   you encompass us with love.

A Touch of Glory
Lord, touch our lives with your glory
   that we may reach out to others.
Fill our hearts with your love
   that all may see the love of Christ.
Inspire us to dare new things for you
   that we may encourage those without hope,
Open our lives to your Spirit
   that we may reflect your praise.

The Seasons of our Lives

Creator God, in the springtime of our lives,
  you give us the enthusiasm and daring of youth.
In the summer of our lives,
  you encourage us to reach our full potential.
In the autumn of our lives,
  you walk beside us as we reflect on years gone by.
In the winter of our lives,
  you enfold us in your love which will never let us go.
When the seasons of our lives are past,
  you clothe us with resurrection bodies
which will live forever.

To Show People Jesus

By my words may I show people Jesus,
  by my thoughts may I show people Jesus,
by my actions may I show people Jesus,
  by my life may I show people Jesus.

Reflected Glory

Lord, as the sunrise colours the sky,
from palest hue to dazzling gold,
help us to reflect your glory in our lives
that others may be drawn to the light of Christ.

A Shepherd's Care

Loving Shepherd, you lead us
   and go before us, guiding us.
You carry us on your shoulders
   through the rough places of life.
You refresh us and let us rest
   in lush green pastures.
You surround us with
   the shepherd's tender care.
You comfort us when
   we are hurting.
You hold us and love us,
   because you are the Good Shepherd.

Life's Tapestry

From the tangle of our lives,
you can weave the perfect tapestry
of our joys and sorrows,
our successes and failures,
our achievements and unfulfilled dreams.

Lifelong Praise

In the rising and the setting of the sun,
   may we praise you.
In the waxing and the waning of the moon,
   may we praise you.
In the ebbing and the flowing of the tide,
   may we praise you,
In the beginning and the ending of our lives,
   may we praise you.

Shepherd-King

As I travel the road of life,
Shepherd-King walk beside me.
As I fall into pot-holes,
Shepherd-King raise me.
As I baulk at the rough places,
Shepherd-King encourage me.
As I wander away from you,
Shepherd-King lead me.
As I walk through the valley
of the shadow of death,
Shepherd-King surround me.

Christ in Everything

Christ in my being,
    Christ in my sleeping,
Christ in my rising,
    Christ in my travelling,
Christ in my living,
    Christ in my dying.

God in All

God in my waking,
    God in my sleeping,
God in my rising,
    God in my resting,
God in my walking,
    God in my sitting,
God in my living,
    God in my dying.

As I Journey
Bless me as I journey on,
Fill my heart, O Lord, with song
As I walk the way along,
Save my soul from sin and wrong.

All our Life
In our waking, be blessing us,
in our journeying, be keeping us,
in our working, be helping us,
in our sleeping, be watching us,
in our living, be guiding us,
in our dying, be receiving us.

The Fragility of Life
How fragile life is –
easily snuffed out
like a candle in the wind –
fleeting, its end unknowable.
Help us to value our lives
and use our time wisely –
and to your glory.

Death Comes

Death comes silently –
slowly for some
with sudden swiftness for others,
yet unavoidable – certain.
However long or short
our span of life,
the last great enemy,
yet conquered by your Resurrection.
Lord, teach us to number our days
and so apply our hearts to wisdom.

For Patience

Give Me Patience
Give me patience, Lord,
　to listen to your voice,
to wait for you to act.
　Save me from impatience
and from wanting to run ahead
　of your timing for me.

More like Jesus
Lord, help me to have more patience,
less prone to get hurt and vexed,
more willing to be kind and thoughtful,
less ready to be so perplexed.

Less harsh in my judgement of others
to see them as children of God,
less ready to seek to be noticed,
more humble like Jesus, my Lord.

For God's Assurance

Ask, Seek, Knock
May we ask according to your will,
not according to our desires,
for you will give us what is right for us.
May we seek you as the pearl of great price,
not half-heartedly but with our whole being,
for you are always present, ready to be found.
May we knock on the door of heaven,
not fearfully, but as inheritors of your kingdom,
for your ears are ever open to the cries of your children.

Called by Name
You have called me by name
and I am yours.
The very hairs of my head are numbered,
even to hoar-hairs will you carry me.
Help me to rest secure in your love.

You Quiet Me

In times of disappointment and frustration,
    you quiet me with your love.
When dreams are unfulfilled and plans not realised,
    you quiet me with your love.
When hopes are dashed and endeavours unachieved,
    you quiet me with your love.
In all the changing scenes of life,
    you quiet me with your love.

Loving Tones

As music floats across the air,
I come with all my fears and care,
to hear you speak in loving tones
in answer to my heartfelt groans
of anguish, pain and daily stress,
Lord, may I feel your tenderness.

A Bleak Dawn

Though dawn breaks cheerless today
and billows of clouds envelope me
and troubles rise up like mountains
and the sun is hidden from view,
yet you are there, the great Encourager,
leading me with the warmth of your love,
the brightness of your Spirit.

God's Gifts

God of love, you died on the cross for us,
   God of life, you rose from the dead for us,
God of hope, you give eternal life to us,
   God of joy, you send your Spirit to fill us.

Let the Children Come

Let the children come to Jesus,
the starving and the homeless.
Let the children come to Jesus,
the abused and the exploited.
Let the children come to Jesus,
the unloved and the unwanted.
Let the children come to Jesus,
the forgotten and the lonely.
Let the children come to Jesus,
the sick and the orphans.
Let the children come to Jesus.

For Protection

Our Rock
Eternal God, our Rock and Refuge, protect us
when the storms and stresses of life
threaten to overcome us.
Underpin our wavering faith
with the stress-bearing girders of your love.

God, our God
Strong Deliverer, surround us in trouble,
    God our Refuge, defend us on every side,
Shepherd of the sheep, lead us in the right path,
    Light of the world, illuminate our way,
Bread of life, enrich us with your body broken,
    True Vine, cultivate in us a willingness to follow you,
Man of Sorrows, comfort us in our grief,
    Prince of Peace, give us a desire for harmony,
Emmanuel, God with us, now and always.

God in Three Persons

God of grace and God of glory,
  Loving Shepherd of the sheep,
God of love and God of mercy,
  Keep your lambs in safety, keep.

Judge Eternal, throned in splendour,
  King of kings and Lord of lords,
God the Father, yet so tender
  To the ones you call your own.

God the Son, yet born of Mary,
  God incarnate, Word divine,
Risen and ascended Saviour,
  Bread of life, the living Vine.

God the Spirit, the Life-giver,
  Wind and fire of Pentecost,
Give us wisdom, love and courage
  All the things we need the most.

Encircle Me

Encircle me, Lord, for I am afraid,
  walk with me, for I am lonely,
comfort me, for I am in sorrow,
  strengthen me, for I am weak,
calm me, for I am stressed,
  speak to me, Lord, for I am troubled.

Guarding and Keeping

From danger be guarding us,
   from trouble be keeping us,
from anger be stopping us,
   from despair be saving us,
from sickness be protecting us,
   from the assaults of the devil,
be shielding us.

Your Holy Angels

From backsliding and betrayal,
may your holy angels keep us.
From yielding to temptation,
may your holy angels keep us.
From straying from the path of Life,
may your holy angels keep us.
From fear and anxiety,
may your holy angels keep us.
From danger and disaster,
may your holy angels keep us.
From sudden and unprepared death,
may your holy angels keep us.

Lord, Deliver Us
From greed be keeping us,
   from anger be saving us,
From impatience be shielding us,
   from all that would hinder
a life given to you,
   Lord, deliver us.

A Dear Friend
Jesus, Saviour ever near,
teach me now your voice to hear.
Save me, Lord, from every fear,
Blessed Jesus, friend most dear.

Protect Us
From danger,
be shielding us.
From sin,
be saving us.
From sickness,
be keeping us.
From temptation,
be protecting us.
From the snares of the devil,
be leading us.
From sudden and unprepared death,
be sparing us.

When Depressed

Come to Us
When the days are dark and drear,
    come to us.
When our spirits are depressed,
    uplift us.
When our hearts are sad and heavy,
    encourage us.
When our bodies ache with pain,
    rest us.
When we forget to give you thanks,
    remind us.

The Strength of God
When depression threatens,
may I rise up in the strength of God.
When loneliness pervades,
may I rise up in the strength of God.
When worries envelope,
may I rise up in the strength of God.
When fears disturb,
may I rise up in the strength of God.
When tiredness overcomes,
may I rise up in the strength of God.
When all seems lost,
may I rise up in the strength of God.

Come to Us

In the night of doubt,
　come to us.
In pain and sickness,
　come to us.
In troubled sleep and restlessness,
　come to us.
In loneliness and grief,
　come to us.
In despair and frustration,
　come to us.
In the vale of death,
　come to us.
In the seasons of our lives,
　come to us.

God's Care

God, our Sustainer and Preserver,
we commit our broken world to you –
our own burdens we lay at your feet,
the trials of daily life.
We cast all our worries on you,
knowing that you care for us –
and for each sparrow that falls to the ground.

For Inner Peace

Busy Life
Busy steps and anxious faces
   show the story of this life,
troubled hearts and weary paces
   show the toll of fear and strife,
Yet the peace of God is present,
   each one only has to ask
for the strength that comes from heaven
   and is equal to each task.

Longing for Quiet
God of harmony and order,
   I feel frustrated and in a muddle.
Everything seems to have gone wrong today.
   Despite my best efforts to stay calm,
I am edgy and irritated
   by things beyond my control.
Give me a vision of a quiet place –
   a green meadow with a creek
burbling through it,
   where I can be still and feel
your waves of refreshment
   wash over me.

Jumbled Thoughts
Lord, help me to relax.
Help me to put away from me
my worries and jumbled thoughts.
Help me to rest in you.
Calm my busyness and bring your order into my chaos.

Grant Us Peace
Lord, encircle us with your protection,
    enfold us in your love.
Surround us with your presence,
    fill us with your Spirit,
and grant us your peace.

Breathe Your Peace
God of peace,
caress my troubled mind
with the music of heaven.
Lift my broken spirit
with lilting notes borne heavenwards.
Calm my tired body
with the symphony of heaven.

God's Peace

Jostling crowds and noisy places
running feet and anxious faces,
people hurrying, people scurrying
people rushing, people worrying.

Yet amidst the noise and din
we can find your peace within,
peace to soothe, peace to calm
peace of God, be our balm.

The Peace of the Lord

Peace in our rising,
    Peace in our living,
Peace in our sleeping,
    Peace in our being,
Your peace, Lord – beyond understanding.

Love, Light, Hope, Peace

Grant to me, O Lord my God,
the love that never fails,
the light that never dims,
the hope that never fades,
the peace that never ceases.

Bring Peace, Lord
Lord, calm my turbulent spirit,
the whirring of my mind,
the restlessness of my body.
Breathe peace into my soul,
bring quietness
to my troubled heart
and lead me with a shepherd's care.

For Forgiveness

With Regret
With unfulfilled dreams,
   we come to you.
With shattered hopes,
   we come to you.
With frustrated endeavours,
   we come to you.
With unconfessed sins,
   we come to you.
With many regrets,
   we come to you.
With missed opportunities,
   we come to you.
For you alone make all things new.

Lamb of God
Lord Jesus, Lamb of God,
the Good Shepherd,
have mercy on us
when we stray from you
and gently lead us back
to yourself.

In Quiet Confidence
When the stresses of life overwhelm,
in quietness and confidence shall be my strength.
When my heart is weighed down with grief,
in quietness and confidence shall be my strength.
When my body feels weak and ill,
in quietness and confidence shall be my strength.
When friends desert and betray,
in quietness and confidence shall be my strength.
When hopes are shattered and plans fail,
in quietness and confidence shall be my strength.
For you are my Rock and my Refuge.

Lord, have Mercy
God of earth,
God of sea,
God of fire,
God of rain,
God of sky,
God of wind,
Have mercy on us,
Kyrie eleison.

God of strength,
God of wisdom,
God of power,
God of love,
God of justice,
God of grace,
Have mercy on us,
Kyrie eleison.

Forgiveness

Lord, you have removed our sins from us,
as far as the east is from the west
and have plunged them into the ocean depths,
with a sign 'No Fishing Here'.
Assure us of your forgiveness,
help us to forgive ourselves and each other.

Lord, Forgive Us

While some starve, many are overfed,
Lord, forgive us.
While many are homeless, we live in comparative luxury,
Lord, forgive us.
While some have nothing, we are driven by materialism,
Lord, forgive us.
While many are threatened by war,
others have a life of ease,
Lord, forgive us.
Help us to share the earth's resources fairly and generously.
May we seek to conserve and not exploit your fragile planet.

Lord, Forgive

Lord, we have passed you by in the street and hurried on,
Lord, forgive us.
Lord, we saw you starving on TV and closed our hearts,
Lord, forgive us.
Lord, we were told that you were ill and did not come to visit,
Lord, forgive us.
Lord, we heard of your need and did nothing,
Lord, forgive us.

For Creativity / Openness to God

The Creative Touch
God of melody and music,
    you put a song in our hearts,
you inspire the beauty of art and sculpture,
    you make the dancers' movements
seem lighter than air,
    you give voice to the singers' notes.
You want us to live out our lives
    in the harmony of praise.
May we use the talents we have
    wisely and to your glory.

Clear Vision
Widen our blinkered vision
    with new glimpses of your glory.
Open our world-weary minds
    to the freshness of your Spirit,
Soften our cynical hard-heartedness
    with your expansive love,
Unfetter the preconceived ideas
    which bind us,
that we may live in your glorious freedom.

Open Arms
Loving Saviour,
you opened wide your arms on the cross
for the whole world.
May we open our hearts to your love
and our lives to your Spirit.

Ripples
Encircle us with your all embracing love, O God,
that as ripples in a pool,
our lives may be widening circles
to include all we meet.

Give Me Hope
Come to me as the Babe of Bethlehem,
and give me humility.
Come to me as the earth-walking Master,
and give me compassion.
Come to me as the crucified Saviour,
and give me love.
Come to me as the risen Lord,
and give me life.
Come to me as the ascended King,
and give me hope.

Living Symphony
God of harmony,
we hear the music of heaven,
in choir,
in instrument,
in human voice.
May we praise you with angels and archangels
and the whole company of heaven.
May our lives be living symphonies
to your glory.

Shed Your Light on Us
God of the rainbow,
   you give promise of new life.
God of the sunbeam,
   you warm our cold hearts.
God of the rain-cloud,
   you wash the world with your tears.
God of the snowflake,
   you shed light and brightness on us.

Renew Me, Lord
Lord, I feel drained
of energy
of inspiration
of creativity.
Renew me by your Spirit
that I may continue my pilgrimage with enthusiasm
till I reach journey's end.

Fire

Fire to cleanse,
   Fire to purify,
Fire to warm,
   Fire to burn,
Fire to kill,
   Fire to devastate,
Fire to mould,
   Fire to refine,
Fire to regenerate,
   Fire to fill –
as on the day of Pentecost.

The Light of the World

God of light,
Sunlight,
Daylight,
Starlight,
Moonlight,
Candlelight,
Firelight,
Lamplight,
Floodlight,
Searchlight,
Jesus, Light of the World, shine upon us.

Smooth or Rough
A pebble, I hold in my hand –
rounded, smooth, pounded by the waves.
My life, in your hands
with all its rough edges
needing to be ground down
by the great Refiner.

God of Joy
God of joy,
you have given us an abundance
of all that is good,
yet so often our faces are gloomy
and our lives joyless.
Stir up in us a fountain
of unadulterated joy
that your Spirit might overflow from us
bubbling like a geyser from the warm earth.

A Summer Rose

In the garden, Lord, I see
images of my life.
A tightly closed rose bud –
insular and solitary
not yet open to the sunshine of your love.
A petalled rose gently opening
bedecked with dew-drops
(your tears for my hard-heartedness).
A rose in full bloom
revealing the glorious potential
of a life completely open to you.
Lord, help me to be a summer rose,
blossoming to your glory.

In Sorrow

Desolation
Lord, the future stretches bleak before me,
  my heart breaks with my loss.
My mind cannot comprehend
  the utter desolation of grief.
My body aches with many tears.
  Give me a spark of joy,
a glimmer of hope
  in my loneliness and sorrow.

On Eagles' Wings
Merciful God, you carry us on eagles' wings and bear us on
your heart when we are in grief and sorrow. You too have
known the pain of human suffering. You comfort us as the
One who laid down your life for the sheep.

Sorrowful Spring
Compassionate God, the earth cries resurrection,
  yet my heart is heavy.
Golden daffodils wave in the breeze,
  yet I am in the pit of despair.
Trees blossom in abundance,
  yet I am overwhelmed with grief.

Out of the Depths

Out of the depths of misery
    I cry to you, O God.
My heart aches with the pain of grief,
    the utter desolation of my loss,
the emptiness and disbelief,
    fear of the future, dread of the present.
Oh God, help me.

Assurance

In the depth of sorrow,
    I sense your presence.
In the midst of heartache,
    I know you are with me.
In the agony of grief,
    I feel your love.
In the desolation of loss,
    I hear your comforting voice.

Walk Beside Me

Lord, I feel so alone,
    walk beside me.
I am so weak,
    lift me up.
I am in despair,
    encourage me.
I am in grief,
    comfort me.
I feel so alone
    yet you are with me.

In Grief

My heart is as heavy as the leaden sky on a winter's day,
  out of the depths of my despair
I cry to you, O Lord, hear me.
  My head pounds and my body aches
with grief and tears,
  sorrow fills my life,
O Lord, comfort me.

In Sorrow

Comforting God,
you tend your flock like a shepherd
and gather the lambs in your arms,
carrying them close to your heart.
You lead those who walk
through the valley of the shadow of death
and encourage them to rest
in the pastures of refreshment,
where you, the Good Shepherd, will lead them.

For Perseverance

Perseverance
Lord, give me grace to follow you.
    The pilgrim way I would pursue,
that I may walk the way of Christ
    which leads me to eternal life.

The Pilgrim Way
Jesus, merciful Redeemer
    you enfold me in your love,
turn my heart and my affections,
    to the things of heaven above.

Grant me peace and give me courage
    to pursue the pilgrim way,
ever walking closer to you
    till I reach eternal day.

Keep me Faithful
Jesus, Son of God and Saviour,
help me now to live for you,
shower me with the Spirit's favour,
keep me faithful, keep me true.

May I follow in your footsteps,
walking in the narrow way,
ever striving onward, upward
till I reach eternal day.

To Follow the Saints

Help us to follow the example of Aidan,
    the patient one.
May we walk in the steps of Cuthbert,
    the gentle one.
Give us grace to tread the path of Hilda,
    the wise one.
Encourage us to live as Chad,
    the willing one.
May we journey on the pilgrim way as Cedd,
    the travelling one.

You are our Rock

Lord, help us to build on rock not sand.
When life's storms prevail,
    keep our faith firm.
When disappointments come,
    keep our faith firm.
When illness strikes,
    keep our faith firm.
When sorrow overwhelms,
    keep our faith firm.
When temptation assails,
    keep our faith firm.
May we build our lives on you, our Rock.

Keep Us Holy

God of time and God of space,
show the brightness of your face.
Help us run this earthly race,
keep us holy by your grace.

Give us Grace

Long suffering God,
you have infinite patience with your wayward children.
We fail you so often by our words and actions.
Give us grace to walk in your way
in joyful obedience to your will,
that we may please you in the living of our lives.

Looking to Jesus

Jesus, Lamb of God, Redeemer,
take the wrongs that I have done.
Jesus, Son of God and Saviour,
help me now the race to run.

Looking only to you, Jesus,
till I gain the prize at last,
Bless me now, O Lord most holy,
keep me strong and hold me fast.

The Vine

Lord, you are the Vine
into which we the branches are grafted.
Without you we can do nothing worthwhile.
Help us to abide in you
that we might bear much fruit to your glory.

In Praise

Unchanging God
Lord of love and power and glory,
   may we praise your holy name,
God of faith and gospel story,
   yesterday, today the same.

God of peace and God of justice,
   may we seek to show your love,
ever searching, ever journeying
   till we reach our home above.

Infinite God
High King of heaven,
   your dominions are numberless,
your power infinite,
   your ways are beyond our understanding.
You are without beginning and without end,
   yet you humbled yourself and came to earth
to be born as a tiny baby – vulnerable,
   yet King of kings and Lord of lords.
At the end of the world,
   you will return in glory –
the High King of heaven.

The Name of God

Join all the glorious names and praise his name always,
Wonderful Counsellor, Mighty God, everlasting Father,
Prince of peace, the Lamb of God, the Suffering Servant,
the Bread of Life, the True Vine, the Living Water,
Emmanuel, Jesus, the Saviour, Master, Man of Sorrows
The Christ, the Son of God, Son of Man, the Good
Shepherd, the Way, the Truth, the Life, the Anointed One,
the Door, the Light of the world, Messiah, Root of Jesse,
Key of David, the Lord, the Word, God incarnate, King of
kings and Lord of lords, the Alpha and the Omega.

Timeless God

God of history,
help us to learn from past failures.
God of integrity,
help us to be transparent in our dealings.
God of eternity,
help us to realise a day in your sight
is like a thousand years.
God of infinity,
help us to know that you are
without beginning and without end.

Praise Him

Praise God in the church,
praise him in our homes,
praise him as we travel,
by road, sea or air,
praise him in the daily routine,
praise him with every fibre of our being.

Welcoming God

For the homeless and the refugee,
God of the welcoming arms, we pray.
For the hungry and the starving,
God of the welcoming arms, we pray.
For the unloved and the lonely,
God of the welcoming arms, we pray.
For the abused and the exploited,
God of the welcoming arms, we pray.
For the sick and those in pain,
God of the welcoming arms, we pray.
For the bereaved and those in grief,
God of the welcoming arms, we pray.

In Thanksgiving

Contentment
Lord, when I'm contented and cosy
curled up like a kitten,
may I remember the homeless.
When I've enjoyed a meal
on a cold winter's evening,
may I remember the hungry.
When I snuggle up in a soft warm bed
while the wind howls outside,
may I remember the refugee.
Help me to count the blessings you have given.
Give me a willingness to share with others
the good things you have lavished on me.

A Perfect Day
Rippling water, lapping waves,
clear blue sky and rocky caves,
Soft breeze blowing on my face
as the cliff-top path I trace
with my dog, my faithful friend,
homeward now our way we wend.

For God's Guidance

Go Before Us
Loving God, you go before us to encourage us,
and come behind us picking up the pieces
of our broken lives.
May we know your all-pervading presence
surrounding us.

The Still Small Voice
Lord God, refresh us with living water,
illuminate our path with your light,
speak to us with the still small voice
and calm the storms of our lives with your peace.

Simeon's Farewell
Lord, now let your servant go in peace,
for I have seen your promise come to fruition,
with my own eyes I have beheld
the Saviour of all nations –
a light for this dark world
and the glory of your chosen people.
Let me now depart in your peace.
(Based on the *Nunc Dimittis*)

A Willing Servant
Lord, how often I disown you
as Simon Peter did.
Help me to witness for you
and speak as I am bid.

Lord, give to me the courage
to walk the narrow way.
Help me to follow bravely
and guide my steps, I pray.

Help me to serve and honour
the God I call my Lord.
Make me your willing servant
and faithful to your word.

The Lord is my Shepherd
Be my Shepherd, Lord, and lead me
in the pastures green,
beside the still waters of reflection.
For there I need nothing,
except the knowledge that you are with me,
guiding me through the rough places of life.
Even in the dark vale of death itself,
you spread a table of refreshment for me
and make me welcome with the oil of comfort
anointing my soul.
Without a doubt you will walk with me
and lead me into your own home.

Lead Us, Father
God of peace and God of mercy,
hear your servants as we pray.
Lead us, loving Father, lead us
as we walk the pilgrim way.

God of love and God of justice,
may we listen to your voice.
Guide us, heavenly Father, guide us
as we praise you and rejoice.

Lead me
God with me stay
this day and every day,
lead me along the way,
protect me from the fray
and hear me when I pray,
help me to always say, your will be done.

A Refuge
Be a lamp to light my way,
be a Shepherd to direct my path,
be a guiding star above me,
be a refuge to protect me.

Jesus Guide Me
Jesus, Son of God and Saviour
be a friend to me,
ever guiding and directing
till your blessed face I see.

Jesus, Crucified Redeemer,
lead me in the narrow way,
walk before me, loving Shepherd,
keep me safe both night and day.

Christ the Shepherd
Jesus, Son of God, Redeemer
of the world and of my soul,
you alone, our loving Saviour,
only you can make us whole.

Jesus, Son of God, the Shepherd
seeking out your wandering sheep,
lead us through the rocky places,
guard us now, in safety keep.

Caring for Others

Sharing
By our thoughtful deeds,
may we be Christ to others.
By our kind words,
may we be Christ to others.
By our loving care,
may we be Christ to others.
By our patient listening,
may we be Christ to others.
By our willingness to go the extra mile,
may we be Christ to others.

Walking with Others
Lord, help us to put our feet in the other person's shoes
that we may share their path of sorrow and pain,
for we cannot understand their situation
until we have walked in their footsteps.

Love Kindled
Kindle love in our hearts, O God –
   for our neighbours,
   our friends,
   our families,
and even our enemies.

A Deed of Kindness
What can I do to brighten
this sad old world today ?
Perhaps a deed of kindness
to someone on the way,
a moment spent in listening,
a friendly spoken word,
the time to stop and be there
and tend the cry that's heard.

The Marriage of the Lamb
Lord Jesus, you brought joy
to the marriage at Cana,
by turning water into wine.
May our homes be places
of welcome and hospitality,
and finally when we sit down
at the heavenly wedding banquet,
may we rejoice with great joy
at the marriage of the Lamb.

Lord, use Us
Lord, use our hands to touch with tenderness,
use our feet to walk in your way,
use our lips to speak a kind word,
use our eyes to see Christ in those we meet,
use our hearts to love with your compassion.

Help Me Share

God of love and joyfulness,
God of peace and tenderness,
God of grace and hopefulness,
God of care and kindliness,
fill my heart with gentleness,
help me show your thoughtfulness.

In Joy or Pain

O God, the source of the world's joy
and the bearer of its pain,
we pray for those who have cause for celebration.
May they give thanks to you for their happiness.
For those bearing their own sadness,
may they find in your presence, reassurance and peace.

For Loved Ones

For our loved ones, Lord, we pray,
keep them in your care each day.
You will ever with them stay
as they walk the pilgrim way.

Freely Give

God, touch our hearts with generosity that we may be willing to share the world's wealth with those in poverty, food with those who are hungry, clothing with those who are naked and shelter with those who have none. As we have freely received from your bountiful abundance, so may we freely give.

For the Church

Let Your Light Shine
On the newly baptised,
   let your light shine.
On those preparing for Confirmation,
   let your light shine.
On those testing their vocation,
   let your light shine.
On those seeking Ordination,
   let your light shine.
On all Christians in their daily ministry,
   let your light shine.

For Your Church, We Pray
Lord, for your church we intercede,
in its sad divisions.
Lord, for your church we intercede,
in its coldness and apathy.
Lord, for your church we intercede,
in its failure to live by your word.
Lord, for your church we intercede,
in its lack of showing the love of Christ,
Lord, for your church we intercede.

For World Peace

Peace in our World
Prince of Peace,
you came to bring peace beyond our understanding.
Yet still we fight with warring madness.
You died for us, but still we will not hear.
May we seek peace in our world, our nation,
our community, our family and in our hearts.

Your Kingdom Come
Jesus, you are the Man of Sorrows,
well acquainted with our grief.
Your heart still breaks at the world's suffering.
Hasten the time when your kingdom comes
and your reign of peace begins.

Bind Up and Heal
Living Lord, pour the myrrh of your Passion
on the world's suffering,
bind up its brokenness
and heal its divisions.

Peace for the World
For the peace of the world we pray
when the Lord himself
will settle disputes between nations,
and they will turn their swords into ploughshares,
and not train for war anymore.
Creation will be in harmony
and the wolf and the lamb will live together
and the leopard will rest with the goat
and the cow and the bear will share
the same food trough
and a little child will lead them.
O pray for the peace of Jerusalem.

For The Leaders
Almighty God, we pray for the leaders of the nations.
May they have a genuine desire to work for peace,
a willingness to listen to what others have to say
and a real commitment
to govern with justice and integrity.
May they ever be mindful of their accountability to you.

Eucharist

Sacrament of Love
Saviour Christ, you invite us
to share this sacrament of your Body and Blood.
You welcome us sinners to sit
at your table of communion and reconciliation.
You yourself are the host offering bread and wine.

Bread is Broken
Bread is broken,
wine is given,
sins confessed
and hope restored.

Bread is broken,
wine is given,
symbols of
the Risen Lord.

You Feed Us
God of the harvest,
    you nourish us with the Bread of Life
and quench our thirst with the cup of salvation.
    You give us life,
you give us love,
    you give us yourself in bread and wine.
Help us to share your love.

Eucharist

'The Lord is here.
His Spirit is with us.'

   Here bread is broken
and the wine outpoured,
   to symbolise for us
the Blood and Body of the Lord.

   Here prayers are offered
and our faith restored.

   Here we connect with heaven
and the Risen Lord.

This Holy Sacrament

God of our salvation, we thank you
for strengthening us with this holy sacrament.
May we go forth from here
resolved to bring your light to those living in despair
and may we seek to establish your peace on the earth.

Bread and Wine

Creator God, you give us our daily food.
You provide bread from the wheat of the fields
and wine from the grapes on the mountainsides.
As we eat the heavenly bread
and share the chalice of blessing,
may we be strengthened by your Spirit.

Creation

Held in Trust
Creative God, you stretched out your hand
and made the world diverse and beautiful.
We have blighted your plan and the whole creation suffers
because of sin.
May we treat animals
with the kindness and respect they deserve
and seek to prevent cruelty.
Give us a real desire not to exploit or misuse your creation.

Signs of Spring
Help me, Lord, to see your hand
   in every sign of spring,
in each exquisite coloured flower
   and all the birds that sing,
in every blade of grass that grows
   and every living thing,
in every tiny newborn lamb
   created by the King.

For Our Faithful Friends

For the unconditional love of our pets,
   we give you thanks.
For their protective care,
   we give you thanks.
For their faithful friendship,
   we give you thanks.
For the joy they bring into our lives,
   we give you thanks.
For those who no longer share this life with us,
   we give you thanks.

Protecting Creation

By our use of the world's resources,
   make us faithful stewards.
By not spoiling or exploiting your creation,
   make us faithful stewards.
By kind treatment and care of animals,
   make us faithful stewards.
By sharing and caring for humanity,
   make us faithful stewards.

Infinite Love

Lord, you cover the night sky
with a roll of black velvet scattered with diamonds.
The stars are numberless, yet you count each one.
Who are we that we should matter to you?
So insignificant, yet you care for us and call us by name.
Not even a sparrow falls to the ground
without your knowledge.
Your love is infinite and beyond our understanding.

Along the Seashore

Creator God, as we walk along the seashore,
   may we know your presence.
As we wriggle our toes in the sand,
   may we feel your love.
As we paddle in the gentle waves,
   may we sense your creativeness.
As we hear the seals sing,
   may we hear your voice.
As birds soar overhead,
   may we rise in your power.

In Praise of God's Glory

Sunlight dappling through the trees, reflects your glory,
   clouds scudding across the sky, show your majesty,
waves lapping on the shore, sing your praises,
   birds swooping overhead, display your creativity,
breezes caressing our faces, tell of your love,
   and all things echo your greatness and power.

Divine Canvas

God of beauty, we give thanks for your creation –
a canvas no human could recreate,
a tapestry unable to be replicated.
May all artists, musicians, dancers and sculptors
realise their talent is given by you.

God of Every Place

God of the heavens, you fling the stars across the night sky
    like diamonds scattered on velvet,
you cause the moon to rise and the sun to set.

God of the earth, you lavish your creation with abundance
    and diversity like the colours of the rainbow,
you make the day to dawn and the night to end.

God of the oceans, you show your power
in the might of the waves,
    in the lightning and thunder,
and yet, you are heard in the still small voice.

Touch Us, Lord

You touch our lives
    with the sunshine of your love.
You invigorate us
    with your refreshing rain.
You stir our apathy
    with the wind of heaven.
You cleanse us
    with the purity of snow.

Your Glory Seen

In the twinkling of the stars and the shining moon,
we see your glory.
In the cooling breeze and the warming sun,
we see your glory.
In the pounding waves and the green earth,
we see your glory.
In parched desert and lush rainforest,
we see your glory.
In torrential rain and gale-force winds,
we see your glory.
In clap of thunder and lightning strike,
we see your glory.
In meandering river and gurgling creek,
we see your glory.
In fathomless fjord and mist-covered mountain,
we see your glory.
In humankind and all that is created,
we see your glory.

A Caring Spirit

Children's eyes alight with wonder,
    give to us that sense of awe,
at the glory of creation
    and the beauty of your world.

Give to us a caring spirit
    for the creatures of the earth,
help us guard and keep and nurture
    and protect their fragile worth.

For Our Talents
Creative God, inspirer of all beauty,
we give thanks for artists,
    for sculptors,
    for musicians,
    for dancers,
    for all who enrich
this world with their talents.
May they acknowledge their source
and may we appreciate their expression.

The Water of Life
Water is precious
    to cleanse, to purify.
You walked on it, Lord,
    and turned water into wine.
May we value it
    in raindrops, in rivers
and in our taps.
    Help us to conserve it.
Refresh us, Lord of Living Water,
    and quench our thirst.

A Father's Care
As a mother hen gathers her chicks,
so you care for us.
As an eagle soars heavenwards,
so you bear us up.
As a lamb skips for joy,
so you motivate us.
We praise you for all creatures, great and small.

All is Well
A clear blue sky
    a gentle breeze,
a lapping wave
    on ocean's shore,
a shady tree
    and soft green grass,
my dog beside me
    glad to share
the beauty of your world.

Fragile Nature
Lord God, you have lavished your creation
with beauty and diversity.
May we guard the fragility of all your creatures
by respecting and not exploiting
the glory of your handiwork.

When Winter is Past
Leaves of burnished gold spiral to the ground
as autumn brings a sense of melancholy.
Birds leave for warmer, sunnier climes.
The hours of darkness lengthen
and the nights turn cold.
We long for summer days and sunshine,
for gardens full of flowers.
We know that spring will come
when winter is past
and with it – new life, new hope,
new beginnings.

We Praise Your Name
Loving God, you hold your world
in the hollow of your hand,
from desert place to balmy coral island,
from majestic mountain to open plain,
may your name be praised.
From fathomless fjord to drought-parched billabong,
from polar ice-cap to humid rainforest,
may your name be praised.
From mighty river to burning sand dune,
from pine-strewn forest to swampy wetland,
may your name be praised.
Let everything that has breath
praise the Lord.

Care for our Planet

Creator God, you made all things
and saw your work was good.
Help us to cherish and respect your creation.
May we prevent cruelty to and abuse of animals.
Save us from exploiting or overworking them.
May we realise they have feelings and experience pain.
You made us to share this planet with them in harmony.
Help us never to betray their trust.

The Sign of the Cross

A beautiful legend tells
how the donkey received the sign of the cross on its back.
As it stood near the cross when Christ was crucified,
it could not bear to see his suffering.
Turning its back, the shadow of the cross fell on it
and so it still bears the mark of the cross.
We too have received the sign of the cross at our baptism.
May we be worthy to be called your servants, O Lord.

A Snowdrop

A snowdrop encircled by its crystal halo,
bows its shy head amidst the snow –
a herald of spring.
New life, new hope,
each spring, a resurrection
after the long dark winter.

For a Child

God loves the elephant and the tiny mouse,
 God loves the birds that fly over my house,
God loves the dolphins swimming in the sea,
 God loves you and God loves me,
God loves dogs and cats, guinea pigs as well,
 God loves sheep and goats – all his goodness tell,
God loves polar bears and lions roaming free,
 God loves you and God loves me.

The Robin

There is a legend told about the robin 'redbreast' as it is affectionately known. When Jesus was crucified, a robin was foraging for insects in the barren ground at the foot of the cross. A drop of the Saviour's blood stained its breast – forever marking it with the blood of Christ. This little bird reminds us of the Lord's constant presence. It brightens the darkest winter day with its cheerful song and provides company for the gardener.

Creation Blighted

Creator God, you made all things to live in harmony :
  plants,
  fish,
  birds,
  animals,
  and people,
but we humans have blighted your plan.
Help us to treat your handiwork with respect and care.
May we work to alleviate cruelty
and mistreatment of animals
and may we seek not to abuse or exploit anything
you have entrusted to us.

Caring and Sharing

Bountiful God, you long for a world that cares and shares
  fairly,
  equitably,
  consistently.
Help us to work for a just apportioning
of the earth's resources,
for honest dealing in all areas of daily living
and a generous spirit
to share what you have given us.

Conservation

Generous God,
you lavish this world with beauty and diversity
and an abundance of natural resources.
Make us mindful of the stewardship that is ours
in conserving and not wasting these gifts bestowed upon us.
May we be conscious of our responsibility
to ensure a just sharing of these with all people.

For the Beauty of Creation

For the beauty of Creation,
thanks be to God.
For its richness and abundance,
thanks be to God.
For its glory and diversity,
thanks be to God.
For the love of its Creator,
thanks be to God.

Inspired by Lindisfarne

To Lindisfarne
A special place, a quiet place,
where saints have lived and worked and prayed.
A special place, a holy place,
where pilgrims come to think and pray.
A special place, a different place,
where islanders live out their lives
and walk on hallowed ground.

This Hallowed Isle
A quiet place, a place of contemplation
   to stop and think and pray,
to ponder the lives of the saints
   who walked this island
hallowing it for all time
   with the love of Christ.

Be Still and Know
In the quietness of this place
may I wait on you,
where saints have walked
and people prayed in ages now long past.
Yet still today the faithful kneel in prayer
and bring their needs to you – their God.
Help me to listen to your voice –
to just be still,
and know that you are God.

The Ocean Wide
Lord Jesus, you calmed the storm,
you walked on water to reassure your disciples,
be with those who sail the seas –
the fishermen seeking to earn a living,
the coastguard seeking to keep the waters safe,
the lifeboat crews seeking to save lives,
the ocean is so vast
and their vessels so small.

Advent

Come Lord Jesus
Come, Lord Jesus, come with justice,
may your reign of peace begin.
Look in love and in your mercy,
on this world so full of sin.

Come, Lord Jesus, come and save us,
with the grace to set us free.
Come, Lord Jesus, come and help us,
may we now your servants be.

Come, Lord Jesus
Come, Lord Jesus, come in glory,
take your world into your hands.
Now fulfil the gospel story,
for your people from all lands..

Rejoice!
Rejoice in this day, you children of light,
    too long have we toiled in the darkness of night.
Today we are closer to the Saviour's return,
    yet still we are seeking this lesson to learn,
of love for humanity, care for the earth,
    peace for all people, new life and rebirth.

New Heavens, New Earth
God of the Advent promise,
you sent your Son to earth
as a helpless babe,
dependent and vulnerable
to walk its dusty streets,
to feel sorrow and heartache,
to be betrayed, bereft of friends,
to die on a cross, derided and forsaken,
to rise from the dead, victorious,
to bring us eternal life.
God of the Second Coming,
judge of all the world,
your Son will reign as Prince of Peace
to make poverty and hunger cease
to end sorrow and death,
to bring new heavens and new earth.

Like a Thief in the Night
God of the Second Coming,
your return will be as a thief in the night,
strengthen our resolve to be ready to meet you
when you come in glory.

For All Your Creatures

To the poor and needy,
come, Emmanuel.
To the unloved and the unwanted,
come, Emmanuel.
To the homeless and the refugee,
come, Emmanuel.
To the sick in body or mind,
come, Emmanuel.
To the bereaved and the lonely,
come, Emmanuel.
To the aged and orphans,
come, Emmanuel.
To those animals, abused and exploited,
come, Emmanuel.
To all creation, languishing for your return,
come, Emmanuel.

Christmas

Season of Good Cheer
It's Christmas, it's Christmas
that happy time of year
with carols sung and bells now rung –
the season of good cheer.

It's Christmas, it's Christmas
the Saviour Christ was born
so let us now all celebrate –
this joyful Christmas morn.

Creatures Worship their Creator
The scene is set, a stable bare,
    a mother and child watched over there
by kindly Joseph, so full of care,
    and animals surrounding the tiny babe.
A cat curls up in the manger laid,
    a dog nuzzles the holy child
while angels are singing overhead,
    a cow is mooing, a donkey brays,
to herald the dawn of the day of days.

Remember the Christ Child
Would it really matter if the presents were not bought?
Nor tables set, nor food prepared,
nor parties held, nor carols sung,
nor trees of fir, nor parcels sent,
nor holly hung and no bells rung,
nor greeting cards, nor phone calls made?
As long as we remember
Christ the child in manger laid.

Christmas Joy
Children's voices sing his praises,
    eyes alight with Christmas joy,
'tis the season for rejoicing,
    every heart of girl and boy.

At this happy Christmas season
    celebrate the Saviour's birth,
word made flesh, our God incarnate,
    come to live his life on earth.

At this time of great rejoicing
    may we seek to show your love
to the sad and to the lonely,
    turn our hearts to heaven above.

Holy Jesus, now ascended
    reigning from the throne of grace,
may we love and serve and please you
    till we see you face to face.

Christmas Gifts
Give to us Mary's obedience,
humility like the shepherds,
the generosity of the Wise Men,
the joy of the angels
and a willing heart to do your will.

King in the Manger
See within the manger lying,
    tiny babe, the King of kings,
Saviour of the world in dying,
    he of whom creation sings.

Lord of lords, yet born of Mary,
    God incarnate, child divine,
with your grace and with your mercy,
    stir and fill this heart of mine.

Give me patience like the shepherds
    to respond and hear your call.
Make me generous like the wise men
    glad to share your love with all.

Give to me Mary's obedience
    day by day to do your will,
that like kind and gentle Joseph
    I may your commands fulfil.

Come, Holy Child of Bethlehem
    embrace us with your love.
Lift our hearts from earthly places,
    to the realms of heav'n above.

Adoration

I kneel at the manger and see the holy babe,
human yet divine – God incarnate,
embracing all humanity.

I kneel at the cross and see the Saviour dying,
for the sins of the world,
his life given willingly,
encompassing the whole of creation.

I kneel now in wonder at the holy babe
now the Risen and ascended King –
My Lord and my God.

Christ the Saviour is born

See the baby in the hay
    mother mild her watch is keeping,
hear the angels sing their song,
    'Peace on earth, goodwill to all.'

See the donkey munching hay
    while the holy child is sleeping,
hear the lamb, the shepherds' gift
    making gentle sound of bleating.

See the cow's warm breath at night
    as it strikes the winter's air.
Everything is bathed in light,
    for the Saviour Christ is born.

Renew Your Creation

Holy Babe of Bethlehem,
defend the children – of war, the abused, the unloved.
Son of God and Son of Man,
encourage young people to dare for you with their futures.
Saviour of the world,
search out the lost, the bewildered, the aimless.
Man of Galilee who walked this earth,
journey with us on our pilgrimage.
Good Shepherd of the sheep,
protect all animals from cruelty and exploitation.
Creator and Preserver of the world,
guard your creation against our wilful misuse.
God of wholeness, Great Physician,
lay your hand of healing on the sick.
Compassionate God, Man of Sorrows,
come alongside the bereaved, the lonely,
with your presence.
Risen Lord, ascended King,
inspire our lives with the example of your saints.

Come, Lord Jesus, come in power and glory,
renew your whole creation.

Emmanuel, Come to Us
In the busyness of Christmas,
Emmanuel, come to us.
As presents are wrapped and cards are written,
Emmanuel, come to us.
As food is prepared and tables set,
Emmanuel, come to us.
As candles flicker and choirs sing,
Emmanuel, come to us.
As carols are heard and prayers are said,
Emmanuel, come to us.
As hearts are warmed by the holy child,
the King of kings and Lord of lords,
O come to us, abide with us,
Our Lord Emmanuel.

Child now Man, the Son of God
Give us grace to see you as you really are,
no longer the baby in the manger, helpless and dependent,
as we often want to keep you,
but rather the crucified, risen and ascended Lord,
who wants our allegiance.
May we allow your kingdom to commence in our lives
that your reign of peace may come to this world
so full of fear and brokenness.

Hear the Gospel
Christmas trees are twinkling,
　carols now are heard,
joyful choirs are singing,
hear the gospel word.

Happy children playing
　wait for Christmas Day,
faithful people praying,
hear the gospel word.

Christmas streets are glittering
　with a thousand lights,
Christians now are gathering,
hear the gospel word.

New Year

A New Year
God of infinity, you make all things new,
yet you remain the same –
yesterday, today and forever.
As we stand on the threshold of a new year,
guide us and guard us
that finally we may attain life everlasting.

New Beginnings
God of new beginnings,
a new year stretches before us –
untouched, fresh –with all its possibilities.
Give us the spirit of adventure
that we may dare new things for you.
May we know you walk the road with us,
in joy and in sorrow.
Fill us with courage to enter this new year –
this next stage of our pilgrimage –
knowing that you are with us.

Lent

Ash Wednesday
'Remember that you are but dust
and to dust you shall return.'
Lord, forgive what I have been, amend what I am
and bless what I shall be.
As ashes make the mark of the cross on my forehead
as a sign of repentance,
so change my heart and my life
by the power of your cross and passion.

Hold me Fast
Lord, of the Lenten fast
forgive my sins now past,
receive my soul at last
and ever hold me fast.

For Your Son's Sake
For our sins, forgive us,
from hardness of heart, keep us,
from Satan's wiles, protect us,
from our many failings, deliver us,
from apathy to repentance, lead us,
from daily back-sliding, save us
and all for the sake of your Son, Jesus Christ.

Forgiveness

For our impatience and selfishness,
forgive us.
For the sharp word and actions done and not done,
forgive us.
For our thoughtlessness and complacency,
forgive us.
For our harsh judgement of others,
forgive us.
For our apathy and lack of vision,
forgive us.
For our hidden thoughts known only to you,
forgive us.
For our hard hearts and our stubborn ways,
forgive us.
For our lack of kindness and consideration,
forgive us.
For our pride and jealousy,
forgive us.
For our many sins and failings,
forgive us.

Shared Humanity
Creator God, you formed us from the dust,
remember our frailty and forgive.
Christ, Redeemer of the world,
you shared our humanity,
save us and forgive.
Spirit, who moved over the waters at creation,
and empowered the first disciples,
forgive our apathy and renew us.

Lord, Have Mercy
Forgive what we have been,
Kyrie eleison.
Amend what we are,
Kyrie eleison.
Bless what we shall be,
Kyrie eleison.

A New Commandment – Maundy Thursday
Towel-girded Lord,
you knelt and washed your disciples' feet –
a menial task
yet outward sign
of a new commandment
to love one another.
Gird us with humility
that we may be willing
to be servants of others
for your sake.

Servanthood

Christ, the Servant-King,
as you laid aside your garments
and took a towel to wash your disciples' feet,
so may we cast aside our pride
and be girded with humility,
that we might serve you in our sisters and brothers.

Easter

Resurrection
Paschal candle lifted high,
Christ is risen!
Choir sings Easter harmony,
Christ is risen!
Organ plays its joyful chords,
Christ is risen!
Prayers are said and hymns are sung,
Christ is risen!
Bells are pealing far and wide,
Christ is risen!
Let the heavens and earth rejoice,
Christ is risen!

Easter Day
Alleluia! Christ is risen!
Christ the Saviour of the world
Alleluia! now triumphant,
Resurrection flag unfurled.

On this glorious Easter morning
sing of Christ the Risen Lord,
now at last a new day dawning
listen to his holy word.

Alleluia! Christ is with us
walking the Emmaus way,
sharing bread, his body broken,
he will guide us day by day.

Easter Glory
The Sabbath dawns –
the day of Resurrection,
bells toll across the valleys green
and down the vine-clad hillslopes
riverbound.
Mist shrouds Christ's Resurrection glory
till the sun breaks through
in radiance and light.

Alleluia! Christ is Risen
Tortured, bruised, denied, forsaken,
Christ the Lamb of God was slain,
risen, glorified, ascended
yesterday, today the same.

Christ the Son of God is risen
Alleluia! praise his name,
Resurrection life is given,
Easter joy we now proclaim!

Pentecost

Open Our Lives
Spirit of God, fill us with power
   as at Pentecost,
widen our vision to see
   fresh challenges,
open our minds to a fresh outlook,
   open our hearts to the fullness of your grace,
   and open our lives to your glory.

Empty Vessels
Lord, we are empty vessels,
fill us with your Spirit,
that we may go out in your power
to show your love to a broken and war-torn world.

Pentecost
Spirit of God, fill us with fire as at Pentecost,
widen our blinkered vision
to embrace new possibilities.
Open our world-weary minds to your energising power,
soften our cynical hard-heartedness
with your expansive love.
Unfetter the preconceived ideas which bind us
that we may live in your glorious freedom
and in the power of Pentecost.

Come, Holy Spirit
Holy Spirit, come inflame us
with the life that makes us new.
Come with power and come with justice
with the love to make us true.

Holy Spirit, come and stir us
rouse us from our apathy.
Come with power and come with justice
come and set our spirits free.

All Saints

Thanks be to God
For the saints of every age,
Thanks be to God.
For those who have inspired us,
Thanks be to God.
For those whom we seek to emulate,
Thanks be to God.
For those whose example has touched our lives,
Thanks be to God.
For all who have served you,
Thanks be to God.

Thanksgiving
Lord, for those who have inspired us,
    we give you thanks and praise.
For those who walked beside us
    and shaped our early days,
we say our grateful 'thank you'
    for all your love has given.
Lord, make us faithful servants
    as we walk with you to heaven.

For All the Saints
For all who have died in the faith of Christ,
we praise you.
For those near and dear to us, who nurtured us,
we praise you.
For those who have laid down their lives willingly
for peace and justice,
we praise you.
For those who have run the race through the ages,
we praise you.
For the 'big' saints and the 'little' saints
who have shaped our lives and inspired us,
we give you thanks.

The Race of Life
Give us perseverance in the race of life
that, inspired by the example of your saints,
we may be single-minded
on our earthly pilgrimage.

Departed Friends
Lord, my heart is very heavy
  for the friends that I have lost.
How I miss their caring friendship
  and their loving touch.

How I miss the days of youth gone
  when our lives were free from pain,
and our hearts were full of young dreams,
  yet I know we'll meet again.

Lord of the Saints
Grant to us the patience of Aidan,
Lord of the saints, hear us.
The gentleness of Cuthbert,
Lord of the saints, hear us.
The faithfulness of Bede,
Lord of the saints, hear us.
The wisdom of Hilda,
Lord of the saints, hear us.
The humility of Chad,
Lord of the saints, hear us.
The steadfastness of Cedd,
Lord of the saints, hear us.
May we be inspired by their example,
Lord of the saints, hear us.

Follow the Saints
Sunlight filters through the windows
kaleidoscoping images of long dead saints
onto the stone floor of this ancient building
where faithful folk have prayed
and worshipped through the ages.
Lord, may I too be faithful
and may I be inspired
by the lives of the saints.

Blessings

God's Protection
God the Father, protect you with his care,
   God the Son, lead you in the right path,
God the Spirit, fill you with his love,
   + and the blessing of God almighty,
the Father, the Son and the Holy Spirit,
be with you and remain with you always. Amen.

Advent
May the Lord who came to earth as a helpless babe,
 strengthen your resolve to be ready to meet him
when he returns in glory,
+ and the blessing of God …

For Refreshment
May the Lord warm you with the sunshine of his love,
may he refresh you with the rain from heaven,
may he stir you with the wind of Pentecost,
+ and the blessing of God …

A Marriage Blessing
God the Father, bind you to each other in love,
   God the Son, fill your lives with the zest of new wine,
God the Spirit, give you joy as you journey together,
+ and the blessing of God …

Holy Matrimony
May God bind you to each other
in good times and bad.
May he enfold you in his love
and hold you in the palm of his hand.
May he protect you and keep you
in your coming and going.
May he shower you with joy
and bless your future together.

For a Child
May the Saviour who called children to him, bless your little
one. May he guide, direct and protect him/her
+ and the blessing of God ...

Jesus the Good Shepherd
May the Good Shepherd comfort you in your sorrow,
may he carry you on eagles' wings,
that, casting all your care on him,
you may know the Man of Sorrows,
well-acquainted with our grief,
+ and the blessing of God ...

May God bless You
May God surround you with his love,
may he protect you on every side,
may he bless you for your kindness,
and may he guide you in your service for him,
+ and the blessing of God ...

In Sorrow

God the Father, who created you,
    enfold you in his comforting arms.
God the Son, who redeemed you,
    walk with you in your grief.
God the Spirit, who gave you life,
    surround you with his presence,
+ and the blessing of God …

Watch Over Us

May your angels watch over us,
    may your saints inspire us,
may your Spirit guide us,
    may your Word enlighten us,
and may the blessed Trinity surround us.

His Unfailing Care

May God enfold you in his love,
    may he surround you with his presence,
may he protect you from harm,
    may he guide you by his Spirit
and may he always keep you in his care,
+ and the blessing of God …

Resurrection

May Christ risen from the dead, give you new hope and the
assurance of eternal life. May the Risen Lord light your
path with resurrection glory and lead you on the pilgrim
way,
+ and the blessing of God …

For the Choir
May God the Father who gave you the gift of music,
fill your lives with his joy.
May God the Son who enriches your way with harmony,
touch those who hear your music.
May God the Holy Spirit inspire you
till you hear the music of heaven,
+ and the blessing of God …

God Watch Over You
May you feel the wind in your hair
and the sun on your back,
may the rain fall softly on your face
and may the road before you be smooth,
may God watch between you and me
when we are absent from one another.

May God reveal Himself
May Christ, the babe of Bethlehem,
reveal to you the mystery of his incarnation.
May Christ, the crucified Saviour,
give you the gift of his redemption.
May Christ, the risen, ascended King,
show you the way of salvation,
+ and the blessing of God …

May God Protect You

May God protect you in your coming and your going,
may Christ be with you in your living and your doing,
may the Holy Spirit inspire you in your very being,
+ and the blessing of God ...

May God Surround You

May God the Father who created you,
Bless you with his love.
May God the Son, who redeemed you,
fill you with his peace.
May God the Spirit, who makes you holy,
surround you with his presence,
+ and the blessing of God ...

Power to Change

May God the Father, who gave his Son for us,
inspire in us a spirit of sacrifice.
May God the Son, who gives us new life in abundance,
fill us with generosity.
May God the Spirit, who gives us the power to change,
guide us with his presence,
+ and the blessing of God ...